MENSA®

EVERYDAY CHALLENGING

MIND GAMES

T0039997

MENSA®

EVERYDAY CHALLENGING

MIND GAMES

—100—
MASTERMIND MATH AND LOGIC PUZZLES

**FRED COUGHLIN
WITH AMERICAN MENSA**

Skyhorse Publishing

Skyhorse Publishing books may be purchased in bulk at special discounts for sales promotion, corporate gifts, fund-raising, or educational purposes. Special editions can also be created to specifications. For details, contact the Special Sales Department, Skyhorse Publishing, 307 West 36th Street, 11th Floor, New York, NY 10018 or info@skyhorsepublishing.com.

Skyhorse® and Skyhorse Publishing® are registered trademarks of Skyhorse Publishing, Inc.®, a Delaware corporation.

Visit our website at www.skyhorsepublishing.com.

10 9 8 7 6 5 4 3 2 1

Library of Congress Cataloging-in-Publication Data is available on file.

Cover design by Brian Peterson and David Ter-Avanesyan
Cover illustration by Fred Coughlin

Print ISBN: 978-1-5107-6687-7

Printed in China

Contents

How to Solve the Puzzles

Anglers Example

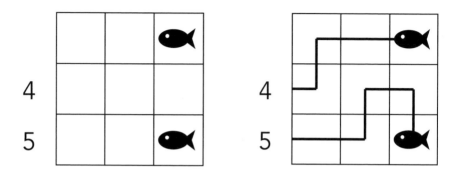

In the Anglers puzzles featured in this book, there are several fishers who have each caught a fish. Their lines never cross, but sometimes they take very long paths through the water. Each fisher is represented by a number; that number tells how many cells of the grid are used by their fishing line. This number includes the cell that contains the fish, but doesn't include the fisher's cell. All cells will be used (except for those containing plants).

In this puzzle, let's start by having both fishers cast their lines into the cell to their immediate right. The line from the 5 fisher must proceed to the right one cell. Here, we have a choice, but the fishing line cannot go straight into the cell with the fish; if it did, the fishing line would only use 3 cells. As such, the path must turn north.

Going back to the 4 fisher, his path must go north into the corner and come out to the right. Since his line cannot cross with the other fisher's line, it will then go into the top right corner, catching the fish (and using 4 cells total). The 5 fisher's path therefore must continue into the rightmost column, then down into the fish's cell, for a total of 5 cells.

Fill-In Example

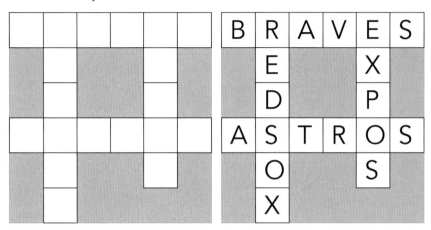

EXPOS

BRAVES

REDSOX

ASTROS

In the Fill-In puzzles featured in this book, we are given words to fit into grids, similar to traditional crossword puzzles. In this example, we have to fit four baseball teams into the grid. One possible approach is to start by looking at the top row. The second letter of that row must be the start of a different six-letter word. The only word that fits in this case is BRAVES. With that added, we can now fill in the two words going down (REDSOX and EXPOS), and the final word going across.

Grid Sums Example

🐟	🐈	▲	8
🐟	🐈	🐟	5
🐈	▲	🐟	8
5	7	9	

🐈	🐟	▲
1	2	5

In the Grid Sums puzzles featured in this book, we have a number of symbols in a grid; each symbol corresponds to a number. You are given the sum of each row and each column, and must figure out the value of each symbol.

To begin, let's compare rows 1 and 2. Row 1 has replaced one fish with a triangle, and as a result, the sum has changed from 5 to 8. That tells us that the value of the triangle is 3 more than the fish.

Let's now examine column 3, which has two fish and a triangle. We know that a triangle is three more than a fish. Since two fish and a triangle add up to 9, this means that three fish must add up to 6, or that each fish has a value of 2. Based on our knowledge of the triangles and fish, we thus know that the triangle has a value of 5. Going back to the first row, we can therefore ascertain that the cat has a value of 1, completing the puzzle.

Kakuro Example

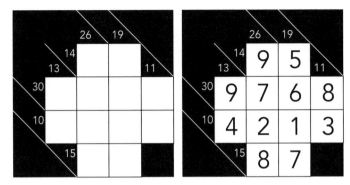

Kakuro puzzles have been popular in the Japanese puzzling community for many years, even before the rise in popularity of sudoku. This is essentially a numerical crossword, in which clues above and to the left of the grid indicate the sum of the digits in each number. The number above a diagonal line tells the sum of the digits in the cells immediately to its right. The number below the diagonal tells the sum of the cells immediately below it. Digits cannot repeat within a sum, and only single digits may be used.

To begin with, let us look at the second row. The 30 indicates the sum of the digits that will go in that row. For a sum of 30, there is only one way to write it with four unique single digits: 9+8+7+6. Similarly, for 10 in the third row, the only way to write that with four unique single digits is 1+2+3+4. Thus, these will be the digits in those rows, in some order. To determine that order, the clue in column 1 is 13. The only way to use a digit from the 30 and the 10 is to use 9 and 4, so we place those in rows 2 and 3 respectively. Using the remaining digits, only 8 plus 3 equals 11 in column 4, so we place the 11 there.

Let us now examine column 2. The four digits must add up to 26. We know that row 2 must be a 7 or 6, and row 3 must be a 1 or 2. We can't choose a 1, because 1+9+8+7 equals only 24. So we must put a 2 in row 3. That leaves the 1 in row 3, column 3. Finishing up column 2, we know that row 2 is a 7 or 6. The only way to reach 26 is 2+9+8+7. So we must put a 7 in row 2. We put the remaining 6 in row 2 column 3.

Now, we know the top and bottom digits must be 9 and 8, in some order. If we place the 9 in the bottom row, then we would have to place a 6 into column 3; however, there already is a 6 there in row 2. Thus, we place the 9 in the top row and the 8 in the bottom row. We then easily complete the remainder of the puzzle.

Mastermind Example

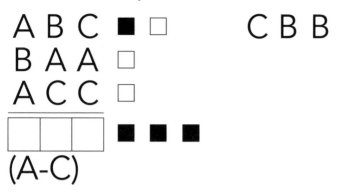

In the Mastermind puzzles featured in this book, you must find the correct three-letter combination of the letters A, B, and C. Letters may be repeated in the correct answer, and the letters may be in any order.

In this example, three incorrect combinations have been listed to get you started; those combinations come with at least one of two types of clues to help you. A black square next to a combination indicates that one of the letters in the combination is in the correct spot. A white square indicates that there is a correct letter in the combination, but it is not in the right spot.

Consider the first combination given. The black square means that one letter is in the correct place; the white square means that another is in the correct answer, but not in the right place. In the second combination given, the white square means only one of A and B are in the correct answer, but not both, and we know it is not in the right spot. Combining the two, we know that C must be in the puzzle.

Looking at the third combination, we know that C must not be the second or third letter, otherwise we would have a black square as a clue. So C is our correct first letter. We also know that A is not in the correct answer, otherwise we would have had two white squares in the third row clue. So C is our first letter, and B is the other two.

Masyu Example

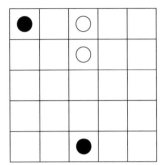 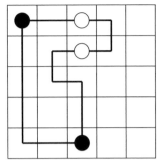

Masyu puzzles, first published by the Japanese puzzle company Nikoli, have become a very popular type among puzzling communities. The goal of a masyu puzzle is to draw a single loop through the grid. The loop cannot cross itself and must visit every circle given in the grid. Each circle has its own special property. When the path travels through a white circle, it cannot turn in the white circle; however, it must turn in either the previous or next cell in the path. When the path travels through a black circle, it must turn in the cell with the black circle, but cannot turn immediately prior to entering the black, nor immediately after exiting the black circle.

Let's start in the upper left corner. Since we know the path turns in a black circle and goes straight in the next cell, we can draw lines down and left out of the black circle going two cells. On the top row, this puts the line into the third cell, which contains a white circle; the path cannot turn in a cell with a white circle, so let's extend that line one cell further, as seen below.

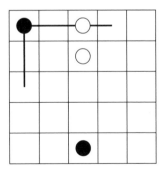

Continuing to look at the top row, the path cannot continue into the top right corner; if it does, then the path won't have turned adjacent to a white circle. As a result, the path turns down. Now, let's look at the white circle in row 2. The path cannot go vertically through that circle (or it would cross itself), so it must go horizontally. We can continue the loop to get to the next picture.

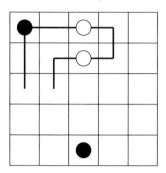

Now let's look at the black circle in the bottom row. It cannot go down two cells, so it must go up for those two. Neither side can go to the right, or else we wouldn't be able to draw a single closed loop. So both paths must go to the left, and we can finish connecting the loop to get to the solution.

Skyscrapers Example

	1	2	2	
1				2
2				2
3				1
	3	2	1	

1-3

3	1	2
2	3	1
1	2	3

In the Skyscrapers puzzles featured in this book, you must place numbers into the grid, corresponding to the heights of buildings in the cells; there must be one building of each height in each row and column. The clues given correspond to the number of buildings an observer standing at that spot can see in the given row or column. Taller buildings block shorter buildings. For example, if a row has 3 2 1 in the three cells, an observer on the right-hand side sees all three buildings. An observer on the left side can see the 3-story building, but cannot see the other two buildings, and so would say they can only see one building.

Let's start this example in row 3. The observer on the left of this row can see three buildings. The only way this can happen is to put 1, 2, and 3, respectively, into that row. Similarly, we can do the same going up column 1. If we now look at the right side of row 1, the observer there can see only two buildings; at least one building must be obscured. The only way this is possible is if there is a 2 in column 3, and 1 in column 2, allowing the 2 to block the 1 from sight. Once we have placed these numbers, we can clean up row 2, placing the 3 in the middle, and the 1 on the right.

Sudoku Example

				1	2
3					
			4	5	
	4	1			
					6
4	2				

6	5	4	3	1	2
3	1	2	5	6	4
2	6	3	4	5	1
5	4	1	6	2	3
1	3	5	2	4	6
4	2	6	1	3	5

Sudoku has become a popular puzzle around the world. Place numbers into the grid so that each row, column, and bold outlined box has the digits, in this example, from 1–6 (although puzzles may go up to 9). Digits cannot repeat in a row, column, or bold outlined box.

To start in this example, we can look in row 1. Where can we place the 3? It can't be in the first three columns, as those share the box with the 3 in row 2. Thus, we can place the 3 in row 1, column 4 (R1C4 for short). Similarly, for the 1 in row 2, we can't place it in columns 4–6 (shares a box with the 1 in R1C5), nor can we place it in column 3 (shares the column with the 1 in R4C3). Therefore, we place the 1 in R2C2 and a 2 in R2C3. Similar logic places digits in R3C6, R4C1, R5C4, R5C5, and R6C3.

If we look at column 5, we know that the digits in rows 2, 4, and 6 are 2/3/6 in some order. Looking at the bottom right box, we see 2 and 6 are already in the box. This allows us to place 3 in R6C5, then 6 in R2C5, and 2 in R4C5. We can then complete the right-hand side of the puzzle, and use similar logic to fill in the left side of the grid to complete the solution.

Puzzles

Sudoku 1

Enter all the digits from 1–9 in each box, such that no digit repeats in each row, column, or box.

1			7			9		
	2			8			6	
		3			2			4
9			4			5		
	6			5			7	
		4			6			3
6			3			7		
	3			4			8	
		8			7			9

Sudoku 2

Enter all the digits from 1–9 in each box, such that no digit repeats in each row, column, or box.

1	2						3	4
3	4			8			5	6
		5				2		
			6		3			
	5			7			6	
			4		8			
		9				6		
5	6			1			7	8
7	8						9	1

Sudoku 3

Enter all the digits from 1–9 in each box, such that no digit repeats in each row, column, or box.

		3	4		6	7		
	2			5			8	
1				8				9
4								8
7								6
	6						4	
		5				2		
2			5		8			1
9	1			3			5	4

Sudoku 4

Enter all the digits from 1–9 in each box, such that no digit repeats in each row, column, or box.

	1	2						3
8			3				6	
7			4			8		
	6	5			1			
				3				
			2			9	8	
		8			2			7
	4				3			6
6						4	5	

Sudoku 5

Enter all the digits from 1–9 in each box, such that no digit repeats in each row, column, or box.

3	1						5	4
		4				6		
			1		7			
9			5		8			3
	7		9		4		6	
8			2		6			1
			6		1			
		5				4		
6	3						9	5

Sudoku 6

Enter all the digits from 1–9 in each box, such that no digit repeats in each row, column, or box.

							7	1
	1	2	3				4	5
	4	5	6					
	7	8	9					
			5					
				1	2	3		
				4	5	6		
5	2			7	8	9		
4	6							

Sudoku 7

Enter all the digits from 1–9 in each box, such that no digit repeats in each row, column, or box.

			4	8	7	5		
		6					2	
	4							7
4					2	3		
9				1			4	
7								5
	5						6	
		3				7		
			1	9	8			

Sudoku 8

Enter all the digits from 1–9 in each box, such that no digit repeats in each row, column, or box.

3				8				2
	1		3		5		7	
		2		4		6		
	3						4	
1		4				8		5
	5						1	
		7		5		3		
	8		6		4		2	
6				3				4

Sudoku 9

Enter all the digits from 1–9 in each box, such that no digit repeats in each row, column, or box.

1	2						7	8
		3				6		
			5	6	7			
3								2
			9	3	2			
8								7
			8	9	3			
		7				2		
5	6						3	4

Sudoku 10

Enter all the digits from 1–9 in each box, such that no digit repeats in each row, column, or box.

1				3				6
	2						5	
		3				4		
9			1	2	3			4
	6		8		4		2	
4			7	6	5			3
		9				7		
	3						8	
5				4				9

Sudoku 11

Enter all the digits from 1–9 in each box, such that no digit repeats in each row, column, or box.

1				3				6
	2						5	
		3				4		
5			1	2	3			8
	6		8		4		2	
9			7	6	5			1
		9				7		
	3						8	
6				1				9

Fill-In 1

Place each given word once into the grid, filling it out crossword-style.

AGAR	DOGS	AORTA	POWER
ALAS	GLAD	DECAY	STRAY
ARIA	GRAB	MANGO	GARBAGE
CODE	OPAL	MANIA	GLACIAL

Fill-In 2

Place each given word once into the grid, filling it out crossword-style.

BOA	DEMO	MOUSE	STARRY
EGO	FLAN	UNION	STATUS
NAY	MOAN	AFLAME	BAFFLED
YES	MOAT	COCOON	BUFFALO
ATOM	SCAR	FLUFFY	MEMENTO
CRAM	TUBA	SOLEMN	OCTOBER

Fill-In 3

Place each given word once into the grid, filling it out crossword-style.

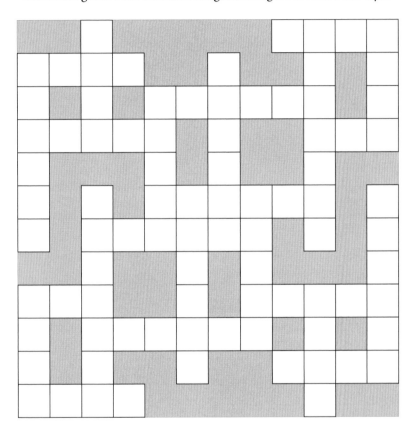

NOD	RASH	OTTER	DINNER
RAN	RING	TANGO	HEARTH
BEAT	SWAY	ABHORS	HOMING
GOLD	YARD	BABOON	THROWN
HEAT	BOOTH	BOTTLE	SCANDAL
RAIN	ETHER	COHOST	WINNING

Fill-In 4

Place each given word once into the grid, filling it out crossword-style.

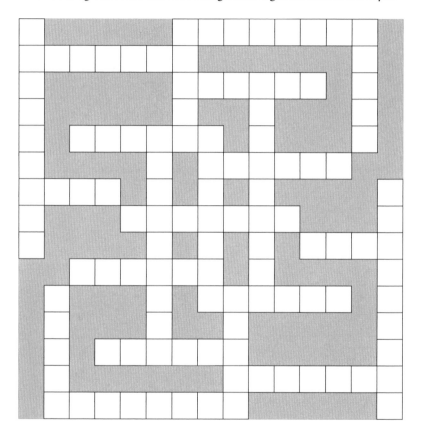

ARID	BUSHES	ECLIPSE	BAROMETER
RAIN	CLOUDS	SCATTER	HURRICANE
ASSET	DEGREE	UPSLOPE	MANOMETER
BLUFF	NIMBUS	WEATHER	PINE TREES
DENSE	RARELY	DEW POINT	
TIDES	SLOPES	FORECAST	

Fill-In 5

Place each given word once into the grid, filling it out crossword-style.

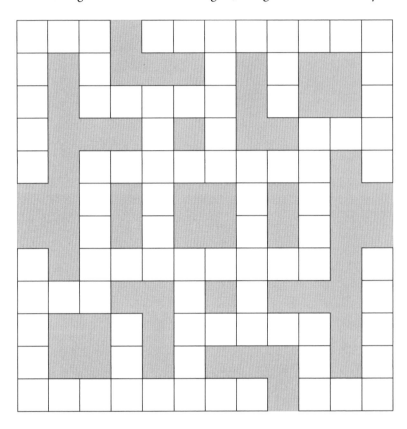

ASH	TAR	SATIN	BOUNCE
EGO	TOT	SNORE	REHEAT
IRE	BROOD	SONAR	CAULDRON
NOT	COUCH	SUSHI	CRESCENT
OOH	INERT	TABOO	EIGHTIES
SIT	SAFES	TASTE	SUBJECTS

Fill-In 6

Place each given word once into the grid, filling it out crossword-style.

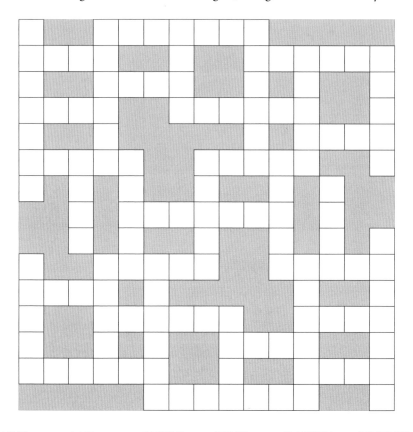

AIMS	LAIR	ALOOF	RALLY	DARKEN	ROCOCO
AKIN	LIRA	DEMON	READS	ENSIGN	RAINBOW
CHAR	NOUN	FORCE	RELAY	LARDER	REALIGN
CODA	ODOR	NORTH	SCRAM	MALICE	REALISM
EURO	OVAL	NURSE	SODAS	NEBULA	RECITAL
INFO	TERM	RADII	AROUND	OUTLAW	RHYMING

Fill-In 7

Place each given word once into the grid, filling it out crossword-style.

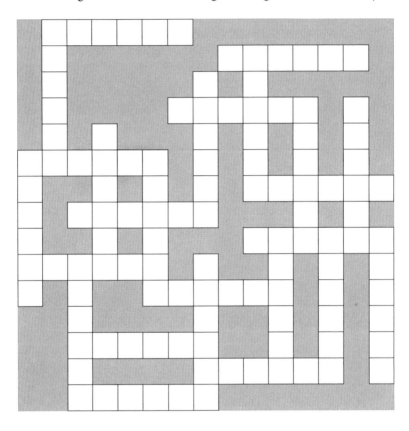

ARABLE	HOMING	RUNNER	SUGARY
ASSIST	LOATHE	SEVERE	TREBLE
ATTEST	MANTRA	SHADOW	YEOMAN
BANANA	OYSTER	SHARED	YOUTHS
BEAGLE	POLISH	SPELLS	
BRIGHT	REPLAY	STATUS	
DOUBLE	RESULT	SUBTLE	

Fill-In 8

Place each given word once into the grid, filling it out crossword-style.

ALIBI	ENDED	OMEGA	ANGERS	GROUND	PARADE
ALONE	EXITS	PRONG	COSMIC	KHAKIS	ROUTED
CASTE	GATED	RELAY	EMBRYO	LACTIC	SLEIGH
CEASE	MALLS	THROW	ENCORE	LONELY	SPRAIN
DECOY	MOUSE	TIRED	ESTATE	MONKEY	UPPISH
EARTH	NERVE	YAHOO	FRIDAY	ONWARD	YEARLY

Grid Sums 1

The sums of each row and column of the grid below are provided.

What is the value of each individual symbol?

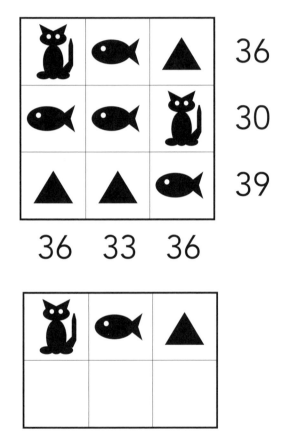

Grid Sums 2

The sums of each row and column of the grid below are provided.

What is the value of each individual symbol?

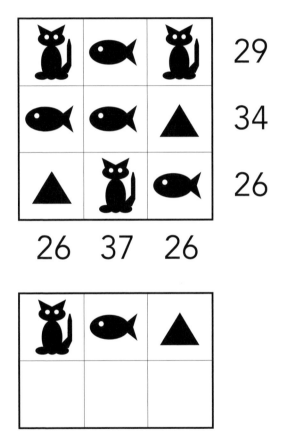

Grid Sums 3

The sums of each row and column of the grid below are provided.

What is the value of each individual symbol?

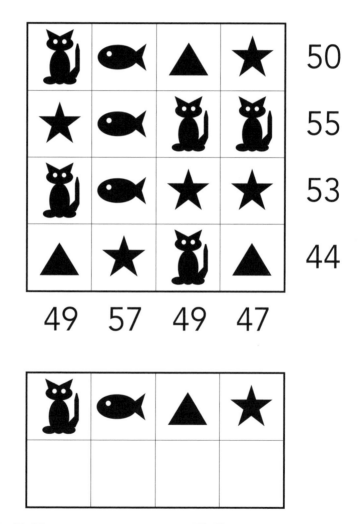

Grid Sums 4

The sums of each row and column of the grid below are provided.

What is the value of each individual symbol?

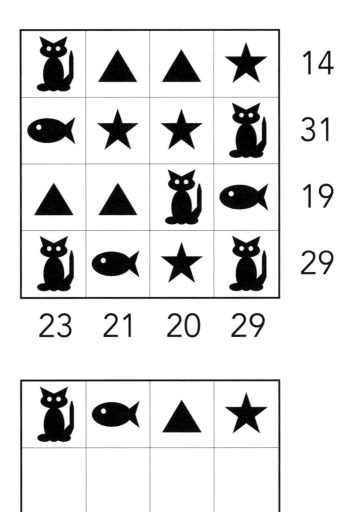

Grid Sums 5

The sums of each row and column of the grid below are provided.

What is the value of each individual symbol?

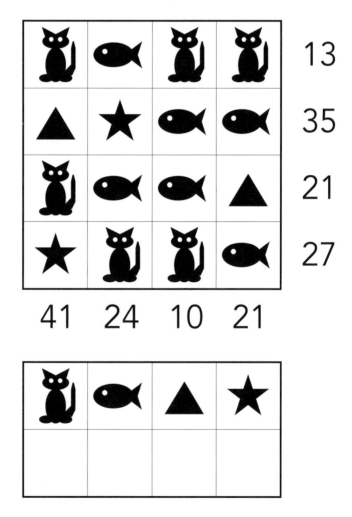

Grid Sums 6

The sums of each row and column of the grid below are provided.

What is the value of each individual symbol?

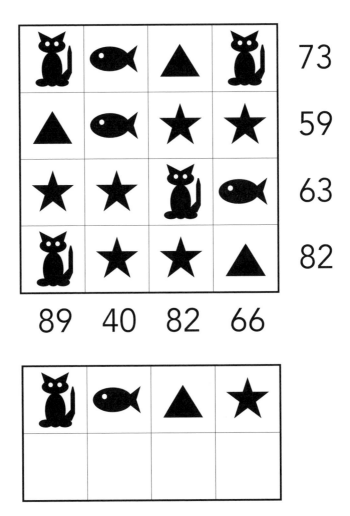

Grid Sums 7

The sums of each row and column of the grid below are provided.

What is the value of each individual symbol?

Grid Sums 8

The sums of each row and column of the grid below are provided.

What is the value of each individual symbol?

🐱	▲	▲	★	☀	**36**
🐟	🐟	▲	🐱	🐱	**47**
☀	🐟	🐱	▲	☀	**28**
☀	★	🐱	🐱	★	**66**
▲	★	🐟	▲	★	**47**
28	**55**	**39**	**48**	**54**	

🐱	🐟	▲	★	☀

Grid Sums 9

The sums of each row and column of the grid below are provided.

What is the value of each individual symbol?

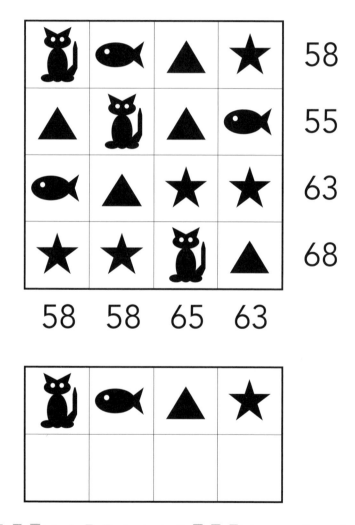

Grid Sums 10

The sums of each row and column of the grid below are provided.

What is the value of each individual symbol?

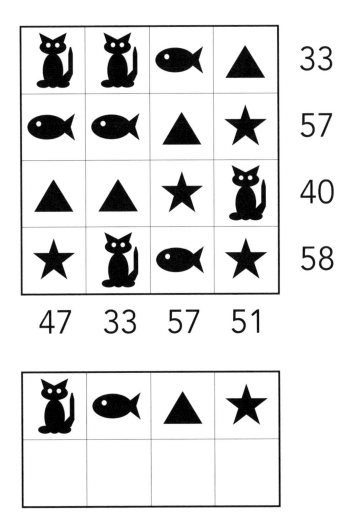

Anglers 1

Some fishers, indicated by numbers (or question marks), each caught a fish. The fishing lines never cross, and every square (except where plants grow) is used by a fishing line. The numbers for the fishers indicate the number of cells used by their line (including the fish, but not including the fisher's cell). Draw the path of each fishing line.

15

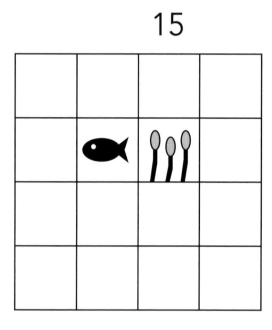

Anglers 2

Some fishers, indicated by numbers (or question marks), each caught a fish. The fishing lines never cross, and every square (except where plants grow) is used by a fishing line. The numbers for the fishers indicate the number of cells used by their line (including the fish, but not including the fisher's cell). Draw the path of each fishing line.

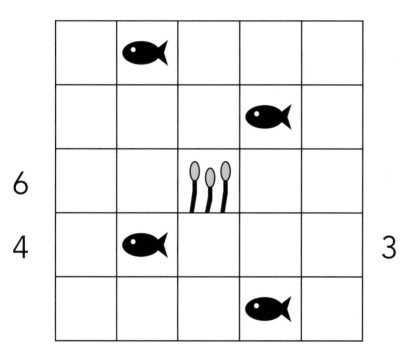

Anglers 3

Some fishers, indicated by numbers (or question marks), each caught a fish. The fishing lines never cross, and every square (except where plants grow) is used by a fishing line. The numbers for the fishers indicate the number of cells used by their line (including the fish, but not including the fisher's cell). Draw the path of each fishing line.

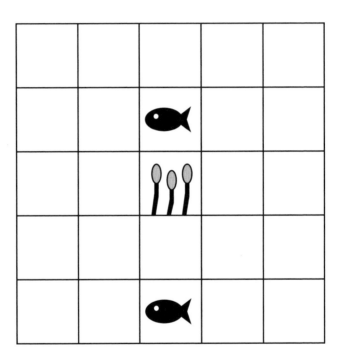

5   19

Anglers 4

Some fishers, indicated by numbers (or question marks), each caught a fish. The fishing lines never cross, and every square (except where plants grow) is used by a fishing line. The numbers for the fishers indicate the number of cells used by their line (including the fish, but not including the fisher's cell). Draw the path of each fishing line.

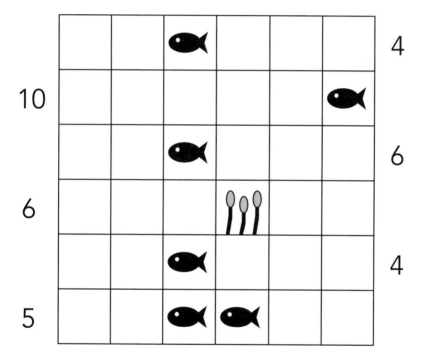

Anglers 5

Some fishers, indicated by numbers (or question marks), each caught a fish. The fishing lines never cross, and every square (except where plants grow) is used by a fishing line. The numbers for the fishers indicate the number of cells used by their line (including the fish, but not including the fisher's cell). Draw the path of each fishing line.

Anglers 6

Some fishers, indicated by numbers (or question marks), each caught a fish. The fishing lines never cross, and every square (except where plants grow) is used by a fishing line. The numbers for the fishers indicate the number of cells used by their line (including the fish, but not including the fisher's cell). Draw the path of each fishing line.

Anglers 7

Some fishers, indicated by numbers (or question marks), each caught a fish. The fishing lines never cross, and every square (except where plants grow) is used by a fishing line. The numbers for the fishers indicate the number of cells used by their line (including the fish, but not including the fisher's cell). Draw the path of each fishing line.

9

2

8

4

Anglers 8

Some fishers, indicated by numbers (or question marks), each caught a fish. The fishing lines never cross, and every square (except where plants grow) is used by a fishing line. The numbers for the fishers indicate the number of cells used by their line (including the fish, but not including the fisher's cell). Draw the path of each fishing line.

Anglers 9

Some fishers, indicated by numbers (or question marks), each caught a fish. The fishing lines never cross, and every square (except where plants grow) is used by a fishing line. The numbers for the fishers indicate the number of cells used by their line (including the fish, but not including the fisher's cell). Draw the path of each fishing line.

Anglers 10

Some fishers, indicated by numbers (or question marks), each caught a fish. The fishing lines never cross, and every square (except where plants grow) is used by a fishing line. The numbers for the fishers indicate the number of cells used by their line (including the fish, but not including the fisher's cell). Draw the path of each fishing line.

Anglers 11

Some fishers, indicated by numbers (or question marks), each caught a fish. The fishing lines never cross, and every square (except where plants grow) is used by a fishing line. The numbers for the fishers indicate the number of cells used by their line (including the fish, but not including the fisher's cell). Draw the path of each fishing line.

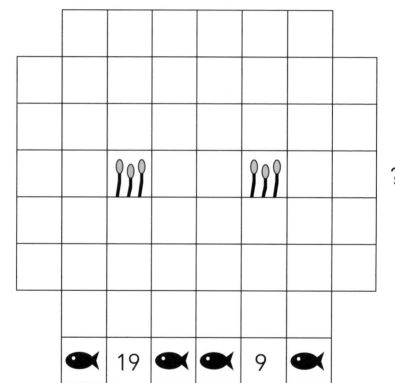

Anglers 12

Some fishers, indicated by numbers (or question marks), each caught a fish. The fishing lines never cross, and every square (except where plants grow) is used by a fishing line. The numbers for the fishers indicate the number of cells used by their line (including the fish, but not including the fisher's cell). Draw the path of each fishing line.

Follow the Directions 1

Follow the instructions carefully to get to the answer!

1. Start with FROG SHOES.

    FROG SHOES _____

2. Swap the first and last letters.

    _____

3. Replace each consonant with the letter that comes after it alphabetically (e.g., C->D).

    _____

4. Swap the first consonant and first vowel.

    _____

5. Add an E after the second consonant.

    _____

6. Replace all occurrences of H with the letter N.

    _____

7. Replace the last consonant with D.

    _____

8. Delete the first two adjacent consonants.

    _____

9. Delete the sixth letter.

    _____

10. Replace the last vowel with A.

    _____

Follow the Directions 2

Follow the instructions carefully to get to the answer!

1. Start with EVIL CHICKEN.   EVIL CHICKEN _____

2. Reverse the letters in positions 5-10.   _____

3. Move the second C to the beginning.   _____

4. Replace all occurrences of H with N.   _____

5. Delete the fourth vowel.   _____

6. Move the K to the end.   _____

7. Add an E before the double consonant.   _____

8. Replace the K with S.   _____

9. Replace all occurrences of N with G.   _____

10. Replace the letters in positions 1 and 7
    with the next letter in the alphabet.   _____

Follow the Directions 3

Follow the instructions carefully to get to the answer!

1. Start with SINISTER.   SINISTER _____

2. Replace all occurrences of I with D.   _____

3. Add an E after each D.   _____

4. Move the first letter to the immediate right of the T. _____

5. Reverse the order of the letters.   _____

6. Swap the letter N and the letter immediately before it. _____

7. Insert an F to the immediate right of the first E.   _____

8. Replace the middle letter with an H.   _____

9. Replace all occurrences of R with L.   _____

10. Replace the second vowel with the previous vowel in the alphabet. _____

11. Remove the fourth letter.   _____

Follow the Directions 4

Follow the instructions carefully to get to the answer!

1. Start with MAYFLOWERS.

   <u>MAYFLOWERS</u> _____

2. Add the letter H after every consonant (including Y).

   _____

3. Replace each letter with the letter that comes after it in the alphabet (e.g., A->B).

   _____

4. Move the tenth letter to the beginning.

   _____

5. Replace the second, fourth, and sixth letters with the corresponding letter from the other end of the alphabet (e.g., A->Z, B->Y, etc.)

   _____

6. Remove all letters that come after S alphabetically.

   _____

7. Swap the second and third letters.

   _____

8. Remove all consecutive double letters.

   _____

9. Swap the R and the letter immediately to its right.

   _____

10. Replace the third letter with the letter immediately before it in the alphabet.

    _____

11. Delete the second to last letter.

    _____

Follow the Directions 5

Follow the instructions carefully to get to the answer!

1. Start with BABY SNOWMEN.   BABY SNOWMEN _____

2. Replace the letter Y with D.   _____

3. Move the first letter to the immediate
    right of the second vowel.   _____

4. Delete all pairs of alphabetically
    consecutive letters (e.g., AB, BC, etc.). _____

5. Reverse the last four letters.   _____

6. Double all vowels.   _____

7. Swap the third and sixth letter.   _____

8. Triple the fourth letter.   _____

9. Swap the second and eighth letters. _____

10. Move the fifth letter to the end.   _____

11. Replace the double letter with LL. _____

12. Replace the second consonant with H. _____

13. Change the first vowel to the vowel
    that comes after it alphabetically. _____

14. Delete all occurrences of M.   _____

15. Replace the first W with E.   _____

16. Replace the first, sixth, and seventh letters
    with the previous letter in the alphabet. _____

Follow the Directions 6

Follow the instructions carefully to get to the answer!

1. Start with HUMPTY DUMPTY.   HUMPTY DUMPTY _____

2. Rearrange the letters in alphabetical order.   _____

3. Insert an E in between each pair of
    doubled letters.   _____

4. Starting with the fourth letter, delete
    every fourth letter.   _____

5. Swap the second and ninth letters.   _____

6. Move the first vowel to between the
    second and third letters.   _____

7. Replace all occurrences of Y with H.   _____

8. Swap the first and second letters.   _____

9. Reverse the order of the letters in
    positions 3-7.   _____

10. Delete all pairs of doubled vowels.   _____

11. Insert a C between the first double
    consonants.   _____

12. Replace the second T with the letter
    immediately before it in the alphabet.   _____

13. Replace the fifth consonant with the
    letter immediately after it in the alphabet.   _____

14. Change the last vowel to an E.   _____

15. Swap the eighth and ninth characters.   _____

16. Replace all consonants (including Y)
    with the previous letter in the alphabet.   _____

17. Replace the first vowel with an A.   _____

18. Replace the first G with a D.   _____

Skyscrapers 1

Place the indicated numbers into the grid, such that each row and column contains each number exactly once; there may be blank squares. Each number represents a building with the given number of floors. Numbers at the edge of the grid represent how many buildings an observer can see from that spot; a taller building blocks smaller buildings from being seen.

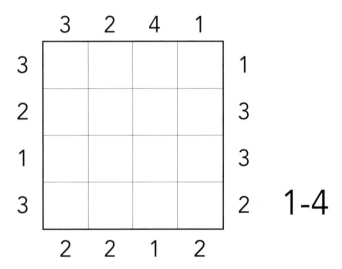

Skyscrapers 2

Place the indicated numbers into the grid, such that each row and column contains each number exactly once; there may be blank squares. Each number represents a building with the given number of floors. Numbers at the edge of the grid represent how many buildings an observer can see from that spot; a taller building blocks smaller buildings from being seen.

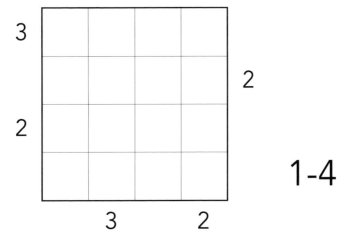

1-4

Skyscrapers 3

Place the indicated numbers into the grid, such that each row and column contains each number exactly once; there may be blank squares. Each number represents a building with the given number of floors. Numbers at the edge of the grid represent how many buildings an observer can see from that spot; a taller building blocks smaller buildings from being seen.

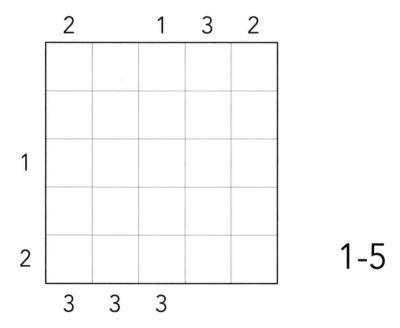

1-5

Skyscrapers 4

Place the indicated numbers into the grid, such that each row and column contains each number exactly once; there may be blank squares. Each number represents a building with the given number of floors. Numbers at the edge of the grid represent how many buildings an observer can see from that spot; a taller building blocks smaller buildings from being seen.

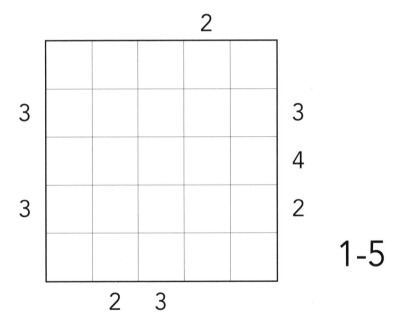

Skyscrapers 5

Place the indicated numbers into the grid, such that each row and column contains each number exactly once; there may be blank squares. Each number represents a building with the given number of floors. Numbers at the edge of the grid represent how many buildings an observer can see from that spot; a taller building blocks smaller buildings from being seen.

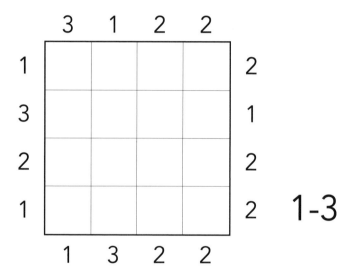

1-3

Skyscrapers 6

Place the indicated numbers into the grid, such that each row and column contains each number exactly once; there may be blank squares. Each number represents a building with the given number of floors. Numbers at the edge of the grid represent how many buildings an observer can see from that spot; a taller building blocks smaller buildings from being seen.

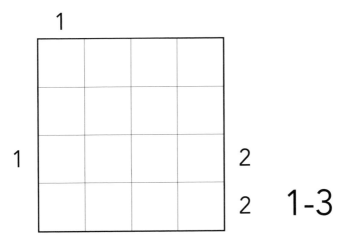

Skyscrapers 7

Place the indicated numbers into the grid, such that each row and column contains each number exactly once; there may be blank squares. Each number represents a building with the given number of floors. Numbers at the edge of the grid represent how many buildings an observer can see from that spot; a taller building blocks smaller buildings from being seen.

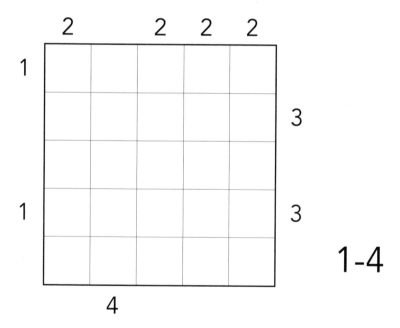

Skyscrapers 8

Place the indicated numbers into the grid, such that each row and column contains each number exactly once; there may be blank squares. Each number represents a building with the given number of floors. Numbers at the edge of the grid represent how many buildings an observer can see from that spot; a taller building blocks smaller buildings from being seen.

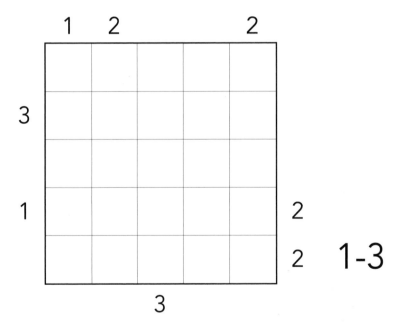

Skyscrapers 9

Place the indicated numbers into the grid, such that each row and column contains each number exactly once; there may be blank squares. Each number represents a building with the given number of floors. Numbers at the edge of the grid represent how many buildings an observer can see from that spot; a taller building blocks smaller buildings from being seen.

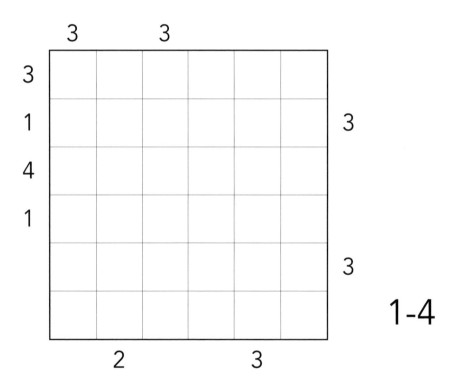

Skyscrapers 10

Place the indicated numbers into the grid, such that each row and column contains each number exactly once; there may be blank squares. Each number represents a building with the given number of floors. Numbers at the edge of the grid represent how many buildings an observer can see from that spot; a taller building blocks smaller buildings from being seen.

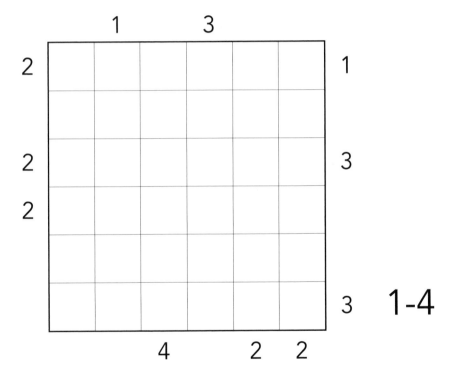

1-4

Mastermind 1

Someone has created a hidden password, and it is up to you to try to crack it! Four incorrect guesses have been made, and you now have some information about the password. A black square next to a guess corresponds to a letter in the right spot. A white square next to a guess corresponds to a letter that is in the password, but in the wrong spot. Below the puzzle is the range of letters that can be used in the password. Using the guesses, can you crack the password?

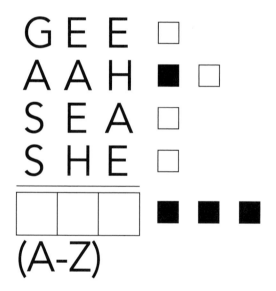

Mastermind 2

Someone has created a hidden password, and it is up to you to try to crack it! Four incorrect guesses have been made, and you now have some information about the password. A black square next to a guess corresponds to a letter in the right spot. A white square next to a guess corresponds to a letter that is in the password, but in the wrong spot. Below the puzzle is the range of letters that can be used in the password. Using the guesses, can you crack the password?

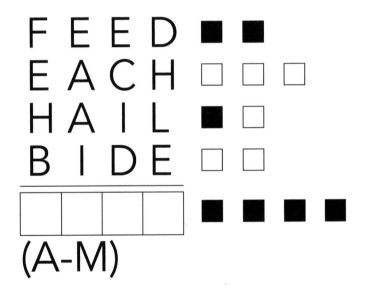

Mastermind 3

Someone has created a hidden password, and it is up to you to try to crack it! Five incorrect guesses have been made, and you now have some information about the password. A black square next to a guess corresponds to a letter in the right spot. A white square next to a guess corresponds to a letter that is in the password, but in the wrong spot. Below the puzzle is the range of letters that can be used in the password. Using the guesses, can you crack the password?

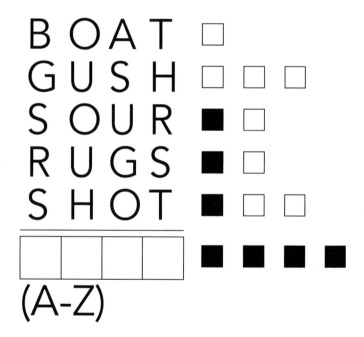

Mastermind 4

Someone has created a hidden password, and it is up to you to try to crack it! Four incorrect guesses have been made, and you now have some information about the password. A black square next to a guess corresponds to a letter in the right spot. A white square next to a guess corresponds to a letter that is in the password, but in the wrong spot. Below the puzzle is the range of letters that can be used in the password. Using the guesses, can you crack the password?

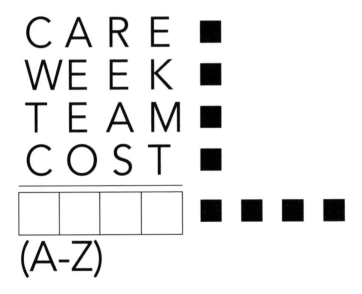

Mastermind 5

Someone has created a hidden password, and it is up to you to try to crack it! Five incorrect guesses have been made, and you now have some information about the password. A black square next to a guess corresponds to a letter in the right spot. A white square next to a guess corresponds to a letter that is in the password, but in the wrong spot. Below the puzzle is the range of letters that can be used in the password. Using the guesses, can you crack the password?

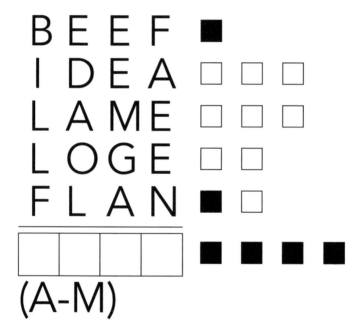

Mastermind 6

Someone has created a hidden password, and it is up to you to try to crack it! Five incorrect guesses have been made, and you now have some information about the password. A black square next to a guess corresponds to a letter in the right spot. A white square next to a guess corresponds to a letter that is in the password, but in the wrong spot. Below the puzzle is the range of letters that can be used in the password. Using the guesses, can you crack the password?

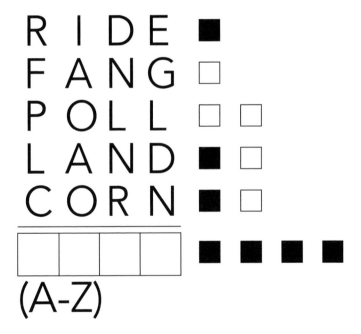

Mastermind 7

Someone has created a hidden password, and it is up to you to try to crack it! Six incorrect guesses have been made, and you now have some information about the password. A black square next to a guess corresponds to a letter in the right spot. A white square next to a guess corresponds to a letter that is in the password, but in the wrong spot. Below the puzzle is the range of letters that can be used in the password. Using the guesses, can you crack the password?

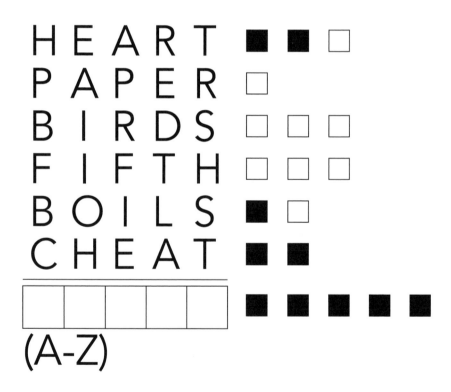

Mastermind 8

Someone has created a hidden password, and it is up to you to try to crack it! Five incorrect guesses have been made, and you now have some information about the password. A black square next to a guess corresponds to a letter in the right spot. A white square next to a guess corresponds to a letter that is in the password, but in the wrong spot. Below the puzzle is the range of letters that can be used in the password. Using the guesses, can you crack the password?

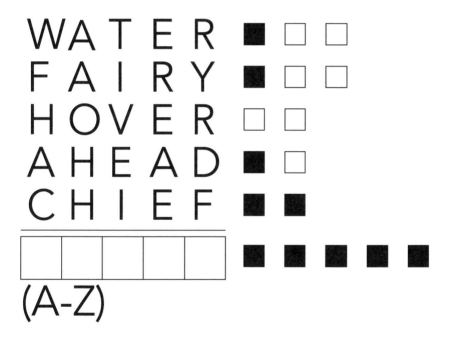

Mastermind 9

Someone has created a hidden password, and it is up to you to try to crack it! Six incorrect guesses have been made, and you now have some information about the password. A black square next to a guess corresponds to a letter in the right spot. A white square next to a guess corresponds to a letter that is in the password, but in the wrong spot. Below the puzzle is the range of letters that can be used in the password. Using the guesses, can you crack the password?

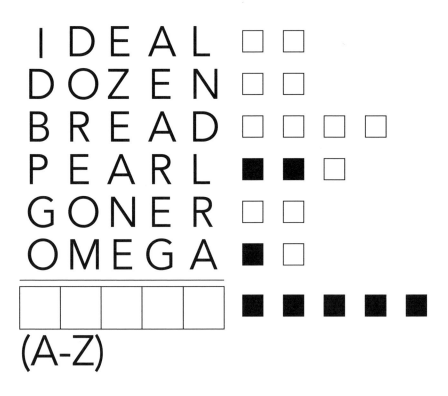

Mastermind 10

Someone has created a hidden password, and it is up to you to try to crack it! Six incorrect guesses have been made, and you now have some information about the password. A black square next to a guess corresponds to a letter in the right spot. A white square next to a guess corresponds to a letter that is in the password, but in the wrong spot. Below the puzzle is the range of letters that can be used in the password. Using the guesses, can you crack the password?

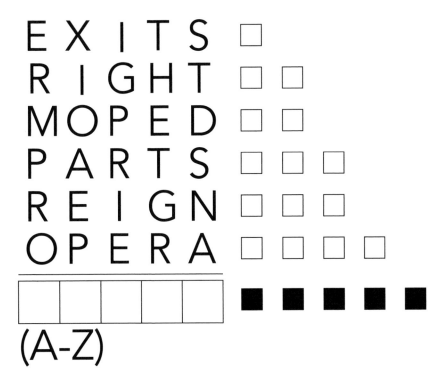

EXITS ☐

RIGHT ☐ ☐

MOPED ☐ ☐

PARTS ☐ ☐ ☐

REIGN ☐ ☐ ☐

OPERA ☐ ☐ ☐ ☐

☐☐☐☐☐   ■ ■ ■ ■ ■

(A-Z)

Kakuro 1

Place a digit from 1–9 in each cell. The number above a diagonal line tells the sum of the digits in the cells immediately to its right. The number below the diagonal tells the sum of the cells immediately below it. Digits cannot repeat within a sum.

Kakuro 2

Place a digit from 1–9 in each cell. The number above a diagonal line tells the sum of the digits in the cells immediately to its right. The number below the diagonal tells the sum of the cells immediately below it. Digits cannot repeat within a sum.

Kakuro 3

Place a digit from 1–9 in each cell. The number above a diagonal line tells the sum of the digits in the cells immediately to its right. The number below the diagonal tells the sum of the cells immediately below it. Digits cannot repeat within a sum.

Kakuro 4

Place a digit from 1–9 in each cell. The number above a diagonal line tells the sum of the digits in the cells immediately to its right. The number below the diagonal tells the sum of the cells immediately below it. Digits cannot repeat within a sum.

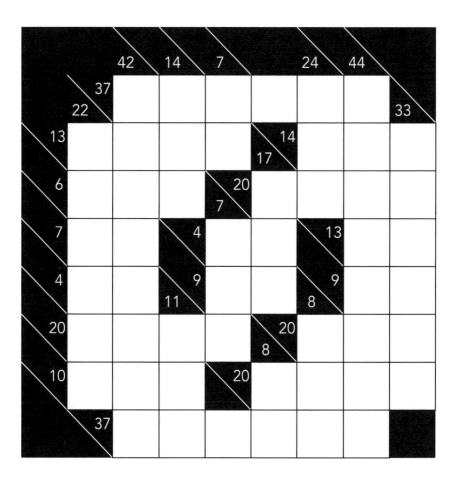

Kakuro 5

Place a digit from 1–9 in each cell. The number above a diagonal line tells the sum of the digits in the cells immediately to its right. The number below the diagonal tells the sum of the cells immediately below it. Digits cannot repeat within a sum.

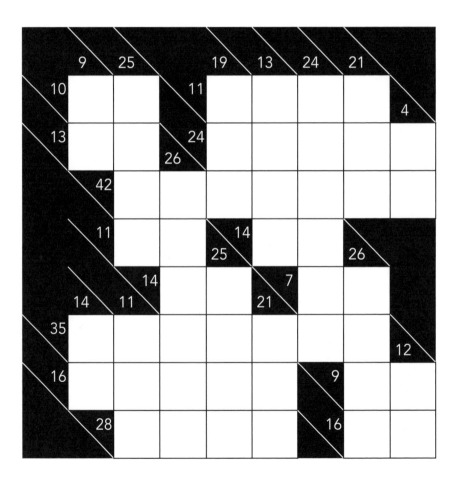

Kakuro 6

Place a digit from 1–9 in each cell. The number above a diagonal line tells the sum of the digits in the cells immediately to its right. The number below the diagonal tells the sum of the cells immediately below it. Digits cannot repeat within a sum.

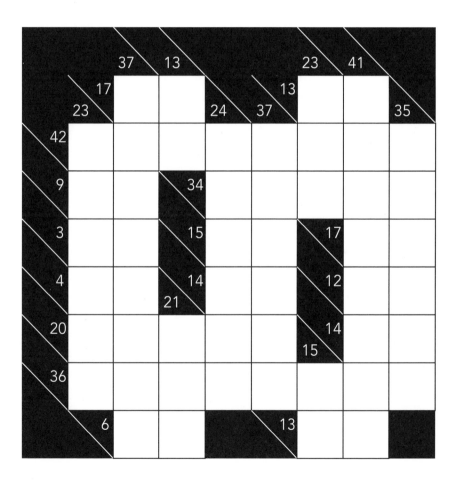

Kakuro 7

Place a digit from 1–9 in each cell. The number above a diagonal line tells the sum of the digits in the cells immediately to its right. The number below the diagonal tells the sum of the cells immediately below it. Digits cannot repeat within a sum.

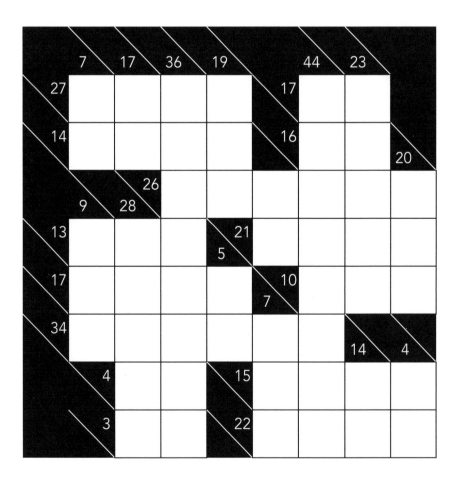

Kakuro 8

Place a digit from 1–9 in each cell. The number above a diagonal line tells the sum of the digits in the cells immediately to its right. The number below the diagonal tells the sum of the cells immediately below it. Digits cannot repeat within a sum.

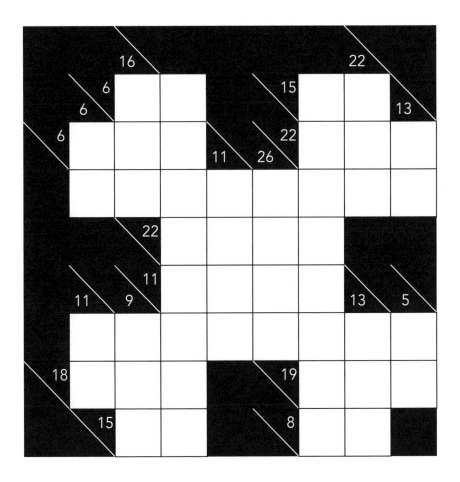

Kakuro 9

Place a digit from 1–9 in each cell. The number above a diagonal line tells the sum of the digits in the cells immediately to its right. The number below the diagonal tells the sum of the cells immediately below it. Digits cannot repeat within a sum.

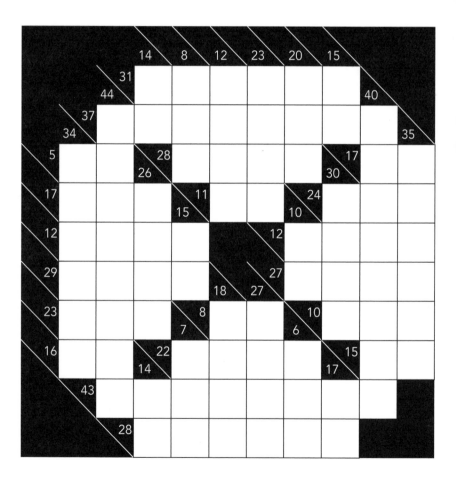

Kakuro 10

Place a digit from 1–9 in each cell. The number above a diagonal line tells the sum of the digits in the cells immediately to its right. The number below the diagonal tells the sum of the cells immediately below it. Digits cannot repeat within a sum.

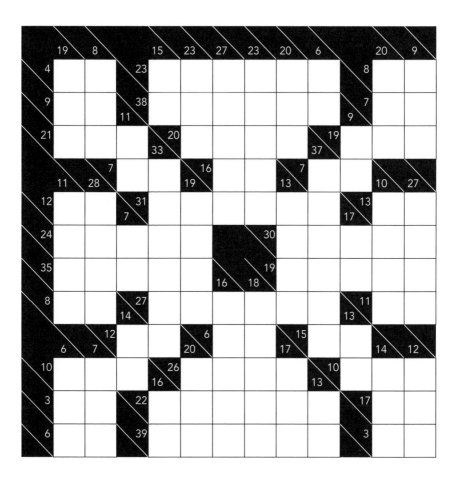

Masyu 1

Draw a single loop through the grid. The loop cannot cross itself and must visit every circle given in the grid. The loop makes a 90-degree turn in every black circle, but it must go straight in the next cell on both sides. The loop does not turn in any white circles, but it must make a 90-degree turn in the square before or after the white circle.

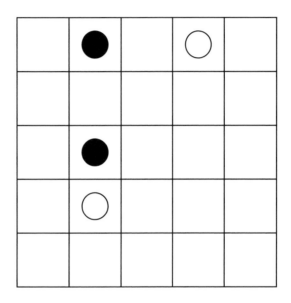

Masyu 2

Draw a single loop through the grid. The loop cannot cross itself and must visit every circle given in the grid. The loop makes a 90-degree turn in every black circle, but it must go straight in the next cell on both sides. The loop does not turn in any white circles, but it must make a 90-degree turn in the square before or after the white circle.

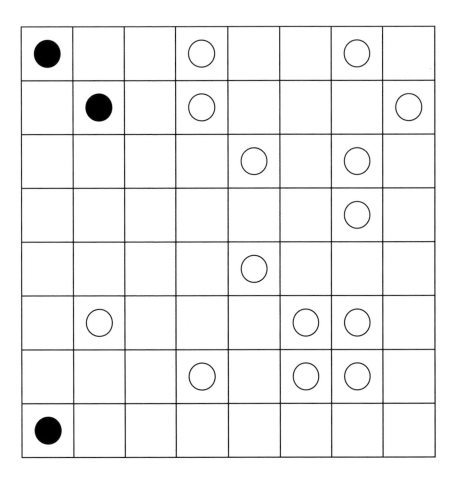

Masyu 3

Draw a single loop through the grid. The loop cannot cross itself and must visit every circle given in the grid. The loop makes a 90-degree turn in every black circle, but it must go straight in the next cell on both sides. The loop does not turn in any white circles, but it must make a 90-degree turn in the square before or after the white circle.

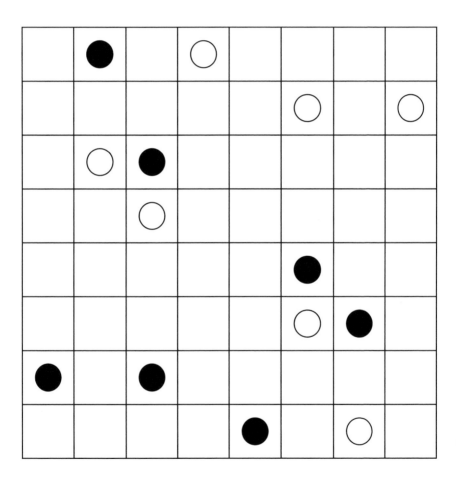

Masyu 4

Draw a single loop through the grid. The loop cannot cross itself and must visit every circle given in the grid. The loop makes a 90-degree turn in every black circle, but it must go straight in the next cell on both sides. The loop does not turn in any white circles, but it must make a 90-degree turn in the square before or after the white circle.

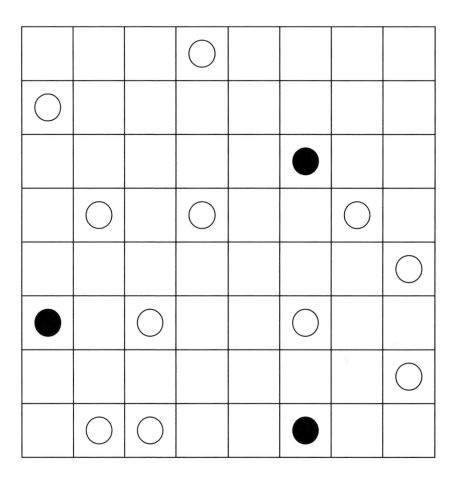

Masyu 5

Draw a single loop through the grid. The loop cannot cross itself and must visit every circle given in the grid. The loop makes a 90-degree turn in every black circle, but it must go straight in the next cell on both sides. The loop does not turn in any white circles, but it must make a 90-degree turn in the square before or after the white circle.

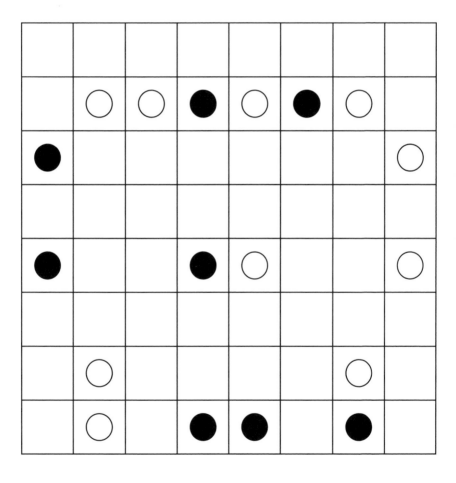

Masyu 6

Draw a single loop through the grid. The loop cannot cross itself and must visit every circle given in the grid. The loop makes a 90-degree turn in every black circle, but it must go straight in the next cell on both sides. The loop does not turn in any white circles, but it must make a 90-degree turn in the square before or after the white circle.

Masyu 7

Draw a single loop through the grid. The loop cannot cross itself and must visit every circle given in the grid. The loop makes a 90-degree turn in every black circle, but it must go straight in the next cell on both sides. The loop does not turn in any white circles, but it must make a 90-degree turn in the square before or after the white circle.

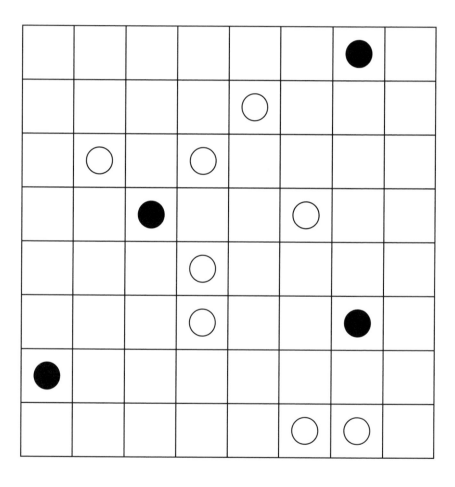

Masyu 8

Draw a single loop through the grid. The loop cannot cross itself and must visit every circle given in the grid. The loop makes a 90-degree turn in every black circle, but it must go straight in the next cell on both sides. The loop does not turn in any white circles, but it must make a 90-degree turn in the square before or after the white circle.

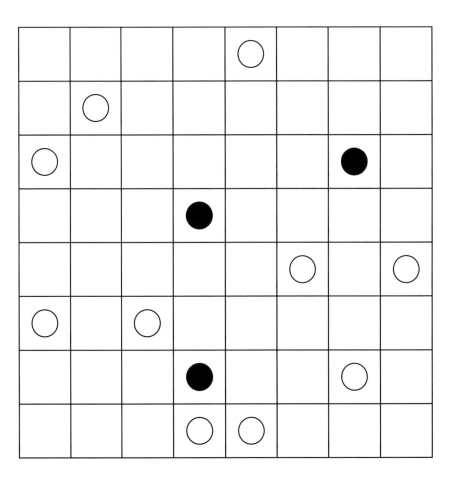

Masyu 9

Draw a single loop through the grid. The loop cannot cross itself and must visit every circle given in the grid. The loop makes a 90-degree turn in every black circle, but it must go straight in the next cell on both sides. The loop does not turn in any white circles, but it must make a 90-degree turn in the square before or after the white circle.

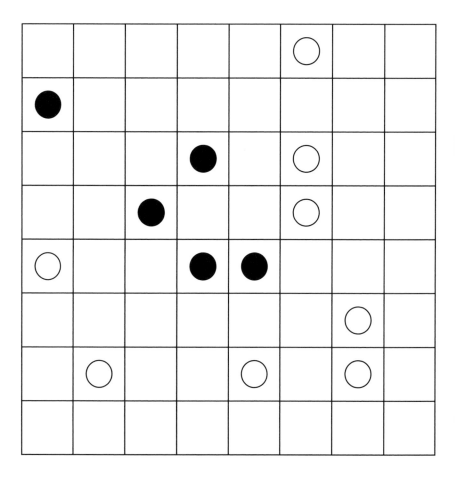

Masyu 10

Draw a single loop through the grid. The loop cannot cross itself and must visit every circle given in the grid. The loop makes a 90-degree turn in every black circle, but it must go straight in the next cell on both sides. The loop does not turn in any white circles, but it must make a 90-degree turn in the square before or after the white circle.

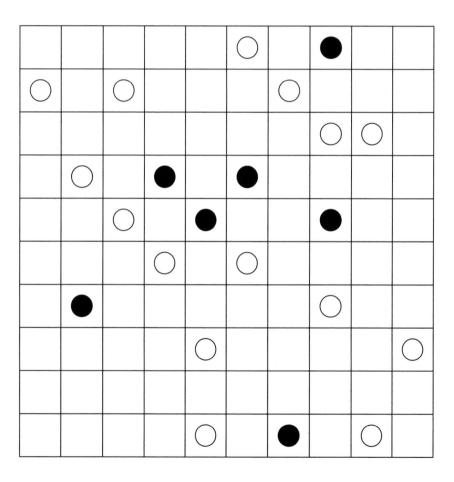

Masyu 11

Draw a single loop through the grid. The loop cannot cross itself and must visit every circle given in the grid. The loop makes a 90-degree turn in every black circle, but it must go straight in the next cell on both sides. The loop does not turn in any white circles, but it must make a 90-degree turn in the square before or after the white circle.

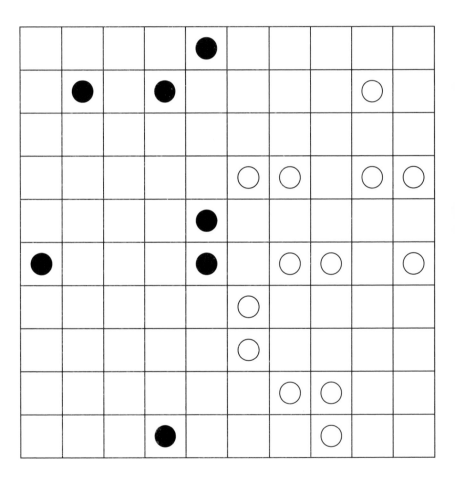

Masyu 12

Draw a single loop through the grid. The loop cannot cross itself and must visit every circle given in the grid. The loop makes a 90-degree turn in every black circle, but it must go straight in the next cell on both sides. The loop does not turn in any white circles, but it must make a 90-degree turn in the square before or after the white circle.

Masyu 13

Draw a single loop through the grid. The loop cannot cross itself and must visit every circle given in the grid. The loop makes a 90-degree turn in every black circle, but it must go straight in the next cell on both sides. The loop does not turn in any white circles, but it must make a 90-degree turn in the square before or after the white circle.

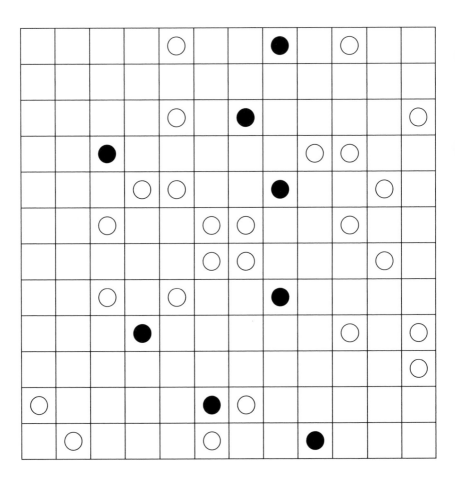

Odd One Out 1

Most of the following words have something in common. One does
not quite fit in. Identify the odd one out.

BACK	RIGHT	FREE
PUPPET	HOUR	TOWEL
BRAKE	SHIRT	UPPER

Odd One Out 2

Most of the following words have something in common. One does not quite fit in. Identify the odd one out.

CONNECTICUT	VIRGINIA	PENNSYLVANIA
ILLINOIS	KENTUCKY	TENNESSEE
INDIANA	MARYLAND	VERMONT

Odd One Out 3

Most of the following words have something in common. One does not quite fit in. Identify the odd one out.

APOLLO	DEMETER	HERMES
DIANA	POSEIDON	ARES
HERA	APHRODITE	HESTIA

Odd One Out 4

Most of the following numbers have something in common. One does not quite fit in. Identify the odd one out.

6	10	15
24	26	35
38	57	77

Odd One Out 5

Most of the following groups of letters have something in common.
One does not quite fit in. Identify the odd one out.

BEF	AD	SH
ST	ENC	SC
IGN	GAL	BL

Odd One Out 6

Most of the following words have something in common. One does not quite fit in. However, each word has been obscured in some manner! Figure out what each word is, and identify the odd one out.

AEGNNOPT	ADEIOPRTZ	AGNNNOO
BHMORSU	CCEILR	EELLIPS
AEQRUS	AEGILNRT	EEHPRS

Odd One Out 7

Most of the following words have something in common. One does not quite fit in. However, each word has been obscured in some manner! Figure out what each word is, and identify the odd one out.

GRN	WHT	BL
VLT	RD	BLCK
BRWN	RNG	YLLW

Odd One Out 8

Most of the following words have something in common. One does not quite fit in. However, each word has been obscured in some manner! Figure out what each word is, and identify the odd one out.

8-15-21-18	4-1-25	13-9-14-21-20-5
25-5-1-18	13-15-14-20-8	19-5-3-15-14-4
10-9-6-6-25	4-5-3-1-4-5	12-9-7-8-20 25-5-1-18

Odd One Out 9

Most of the following words have something in common. One does not quite fit in. However, each word has been obscured in some manner! Figure out what each word is, and identify the odd one out.

DPXCPZT	CSPODPT	KFUT
QBDLFST	GBMDPOT	FBHMFT
SBQUPST	CFBST	MJPOT

Odd One Out 10

Some puzzles in puzzle hunts have a metapuzzle, which requires solving other puzzles in order to get the clues you need to solve a subsequent puzzle. This is one of those puzzles.

The answers to each of the answers in the Grid Sums puzzles correspond to a word. One of those words does not belong. Figure out what each word is, and identify the odd one out!

Answer Keys

Sudoku 1

1	4	6	7	3	5	9	2	8
5	2	9	1	8	4	3	6	7
8	7	3	6	9	2	1	5	4
9	8	2	4	7	3	5	1	6
3	6	1	8	5	9	4	7	2
7	5	4	2	1	6	8	9	3
6	9	5	3	2	8	7	4	1
2	3	7	9	4	1	6	8	5
4	1	8	5	6	7	2	3	9

Sudoku 2

1	2	8	7	6	5	9	3	4
3	4	7	2	8	9	1	5	6
6	9	5	3	4	1	2	8	7
8	7	1	6	9	3	5	4	2
9	5	4	1	7	2	8	6	3
2	3	6	4	5	8	7	1	9
4	1	9	8	3	7	6	2	5
5	6	2	9	1	4	3	7	8
7	8	3	5	2	6	4	9	1

Sudoku 3

5	8	3	4	9	6	7	1	2
6	2	9	1	5	7	4	8	3
1	7	4	2	8	3	5	6	9
4	9	1	6	2	5	3	7	8
7	5	8	3	1	4	9	2	6
3	6	2	8	7	9	1	4	5
8	4	5	9	6	1	2	3	7
2	3	7	5	4	8	6	9	1
9	1	6	7	3	2	8	5	4

Sudoku 4

5	1	2	9	6	8	7	4	3
8	9	4	3	2	7	5	6	1
7	3	6	4	1	5	8	2	9
4	6	5	8	9	1	3	7	2
2	8	9	7	3	4	6	1	5
3	7	1	2	5	6	9	8	4
9	5	8	6	4	2	1	3	7
1	4	7	5	8	3	2	9	6
6	2	3	1	7	9	4	5	8

Sudoku 5

3	1	2	8	6	9	7	5	4
7	8	4	3	2	5	6	1	9
5	6	9	1	4	7	8	3	2
9	4	6	5	1	8	2	7	3
2	7	1	9	3	4	5	6	8
8	5	3	2	7	6	9	4	1
4	9	8	6	5	1	3	2	7
1	2	5	7	9	3	4	8	6
6	3	7	4	8	2	1	9	5

Sudoku 6

3	8	6	5	4	2	9	7	1
9	1	2	3	7	8	6	4	5
7	4	5	6	1	9	3	8	2
1	7	8	9	2	3	4	5	6
2	3	9	4	5	6	7	1	8
6	5	4	7	8	1	2	3	9
8	9	1	2	3	4	5	6	7
5	2	3	1	6	7	8	9	4
4	6	7	8	9	5	1	2	3

Sudoku 7

2	1	9	4	8	7	5	3	6
5	7	6	9	3	1	8	2	4
3	4	8	6	2	5	1	9	7
4	6	1	8	5	2	3	7	9
9	3	5	7	1	6	2	4	8
7	8	2	3	4	9	6	1	5
8	5	4	2	7	3	9	6	1
1	9	3	5	6	4	7	8	2
6	2	7	1	9	8	4	5	3

Sudoku 8

3	4	5	7	8	6	1	9	2
9	1	6	3	2	5	4	7	8
8	7	2	1	4	9	6	5	3
7	3	9	5	1	8	2	4	6
1	6	4	9	7	2	8	3	5
2	5	8	4	6	3	9	1	7
4	2	7	8	5	1	3	6	9
5	8	3	6	9	4	7	2	1
6	9	1	2	3	7	5	8	4

Sudoku 9

1	2	6	3	4	9	5	7	8
7	5	3	1	2	8	6	4	9
4	8	9	5	6	7	1	2	3
3	1	5	7	8	6	4	9	2
6	7	4	9	3	2	8	1	5
8	9	2	4	1	5	3	6	7
2	4	1	8	9	3	7	5	6
9	3	7	6	5	4	2	8	1
5	6	8	2	7	1	9	3	4

Sudoku 10

1	4	5	2	3	8	9	7	6
7	2	6	4	1	9	3	5	8
8	9	3	5	7	6	4	1	2
9	5	7	1	2	3	8	6	4
3	6	1	8	9	4	5	2	7
4	8	2	7	6	5	1	9	3
6	1	9	3	8	2	7	4	5
2	3	4	9	5	7	6	8	1
5	7	8	6	4	1	2	3	9

Sudoku 11

1	4	5	2	3	8	9	7	6
7	2	6	9	4	1	8	5	3
8	9	3	5	7	6	4	1	2
5	7	4	1	2	3	6	9	8
3	6	1	8	9	4	5	2	7
9	8	2	7	6	5	3	4	1
4	1	9	3	8	2	7	6	5
2	3	7	6	5	9	1	8	4
6	5	8	4	1	7	2	3	9

Fill-In 1

```
M A N G O . . . A
A . . . P O W E R
N . . A . . . . I
I . G L A C I A L
A G A R . . O . .
. . A . . D O G S
G A R B A G E . T
. L . . L . . . R
. A O R T A . . A
. S . . D E C A Y
```

Fill-In 2

```
Y . B A F F L E D
E . O . L . . . E
S T A T U S . M S
. U . F . . M O A T
A . B U F F A L O . A
F L A N Y . U . R
L . I . C . S C A R
A . O C T O B E R Y
M O A N . C . . A
E . T . S O L E M N
. O . . O O G . A
. M E M E N T O . Y
```

Fill-In 3

```
. . . R . . . S W A Y
B E A T . A . I . A
O . I . B A B O O N . R
T A N G O . H . . N O D
T . . O . O . . I
L . S . T H R O W N . H
E . C O H O S T . G . E
. . A . . M . T . . A
R A N . I . E T H E R
I . D I N N E R . E . T
N . A . G . . R A S H
G O L D . . . . T
```

Fill-In 4

```
H . . . D E W P O I N T
U P S L O P E . . . . I
R . . . N I M B U S . D
R . . S . A . . . E
I . S L O P E S . R . S
C . . I . C L O U D S
A R I D . N . A . M . M
N . W E A T H E R . A
E . T . T T . R A I N
. D E G R E E . E . O M
B . E . R A R E L Y . M
L . E . S . . . . E
U . B U S H E S . . T
F . . . . E C L I P S E
F O R E C A S T . . R
```

Fill-In 5

```
S I T . S U B J E C T S
N . O . . R . G . . A
O . T A B O O . O . F
R . . O . O . I R E
E . C A U L D R O N . S
. O . N . E . E
. U . C . H . R
T . C R E S C E N T . S
A S H . U . A . . O
S . . O . S A T I N . N
T . . O . H . . O . A
E I G H T I E S . T A R
```

Fill-In 6

```
R . R E A L I G N
E U R O . I . E N S I G N
C . C H A R . B . O . U
I N F O . A R O U N D . R
T . C . . L . A I M S
A L O O F . R E A D S . E
L . D . A . E . L
. O . R E A L I S M . A
. R . C . L . O . I R
S . R E L A Y . N O R T H
C O D A . A . . U . Y
R . D A R K E N . T E R M
A . I . D . O V A L . I
M A L I C E . U . A K I N
. . . R A I N B O W . G
```

Fill-In 7

```
. B A N A N A
R . . . . . S P E L L S
I . . . S . O
G . . R E P L A Y . R
H . A . V . I . E . U
S T A T U S E . S O . N
H . T . U . R . H O M I N G
A . B E A G L E . . A . E
D . S A . . M A N T R A
O Y S T E R . S . S R . R
W . H . Y O U T H S . E . A
R . A . B . . I . B . B
. R E S U L T . S . L . L
E . . . L O A T H E . E
. D O U B L E
```

Fill-In 8

```
M O N K E Y . L . R O U T E D
O . . . A L O N E . . . E
U P P I S H . N . L A C T I C
S . . . O M E G A . I . O
E M B R Y O . L . Y E A R L Y
A . . . Y . . A . E
S L E I G H . . F R I D A Y
L . A . . . . T . L
E S T A T E . K H A K I S
. H . E . S . . . . B
P A R A D E . P . C O S M I C
R . O . N E R V E . . . A
O N W A R D . A . A N G E R S
N . . E X I T S . . . T
G R O U N D . N . E N C O R E
```

Grid Sums 1

🐈	🐟	▲
12	9	15

Grid Sums 2

🐈	🐟	▲
7	15	4

Grid Sums 3

🐈	🐟	▲	★
14	15	9	12

Grid Sums 4

🐈	🐟	▲	★
5	12	1	7

Grid Sums 5

🐈	🐟	▲	★
4	1	15	18

Grid Sums 6

🐈	🐟	▲	★
25	2	21	18

Grid Sums 7

🐈	🐟	▲	★	☼
8	3	20	9	23

Grid Sums 8

🐈	🐟	▲	★	☼
14	9	1	18	2

Grid Sums 9

🐈	🐟	▲	★
14	9	16	19

Grid Sums 10

🐈	🐟	▲	★
5	15	8	19

Anglers 1
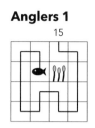

Anglers 2
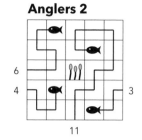

Anglers 3
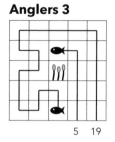

Anglers 4
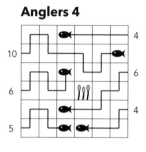

Anglers 5
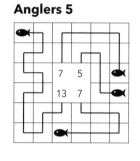

Anglers 6
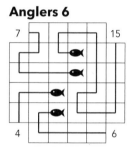

Anglers 7
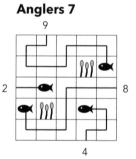

Anglers 8
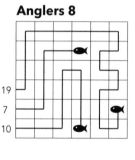

Anglers 9
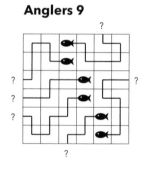

Anglers 10
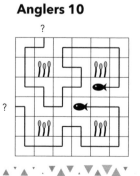

Anglers 11
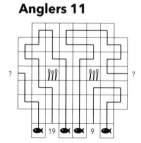

Anglers 12
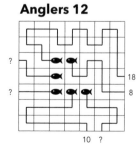

Follow the Directions 1
1. FROGSHOES
2. SROGSHOEF
3. TSOHTIOEG
4. OSTHTIOEG
5. OSTEHTIOEG
6. OSTENTIOEG
7. OSTENTIOED
8. OPENTIOED
9. OPENTOED
10. OPENTOAD

Follow the Directions 2
1. EVILCHICKEN
2. EVILEKCIHCN
3. CEVILEKCIHN
4. CEVILEKCINN
5. CEVILEKCNN
6. CEVILECNNK
7. CEVILECENNK
8. CEVILECENNS
9. CEVILECEGGS
10. DEVILEDEGGS

Follow the Directions 3
1. SINISTER
2. SDNDSTER
3. SDENDESTER
4. DENDESTSER
5. RESTSEDNED
6. RESTSENDED
7. REFSTSENDED
8. REFSTHENDED
9. LEFSTHENDED
10. LEFSTHANDED
11. LEFTHANDED

Follow the Directions 4
1. MAYFLOWERS
2. MHAYHFHLHOWHERHSH
3. NIBZIGIMIPXIFSITI
4. PNIBZIGIMIXIFSITI
5. PMIYZRGIMIXIFSITI
6. PMIRGIMIIFSII
7. PIMRGIMIIFSII
8. PIMRGIMFS
9. PIMGRIMFS
10. PILGRIMFS
11. PILGRIMS

Follow the Directions 5

1. BABYSNOWMEN
2. BABDSNOWMEN
3. ABDSNOBWMEN
4. DSBWMEN
5. DSBNEMW
6. DSBNEEMW
7. DSENEBMW
8. DSENNNEBMW
9. DBENNNESMW
10. DBENNESMWN
11. DBELLESMWN
12. DHELLESMWN
13. DHILLESMWN
14. DHILLESWN
15. DHILLESEN
16. CHILLDREN

Follow the Directions 6

1. HUMPTYDUMPTY
2. DHMMPPTTUUYY
3. DHMEMPERTETUEUYEY
4. DHMMPETETEUYY
5. DTMMPETEHEUYY
6. DTEMMPTEHEUYY
7. DTEMMPTEHEUHH
8. TDEMMPTEHEUHH
9. TDTPMMEEHEUHH
10. TDTPMMHEUHH
11. TDTPMCMHEUHH
12. TDSPMCMHEUHH
13. TDSPNCMHEUHH
14. TDSPNCMHEEHH
15. TDSPNCMEHEHH
16. SCROMBLEGEGG
17. SCRAMBLEGEGG
18. SCRAMBLEDEGG

Skyscrapers 1

2	3	1	4
3	4	2	1
4	1	3	2
1	2	4	3

Skyscrapers 2

2	3	4	1
1	4	2	3
3	2	1	4
4	1	3	2

Skyscrapers 3

2	4	5	1	3
1	5	3	4	2
5	2	4	3	1
4	3	1	2	5
3	1	2	5	4

Skyscrapers 4

3	2	1	4	5
1	4	5	3	2
4	5	3	2	1
2	1	4	5	3
5	3	2	1	4

Skyscrapers 5

	3	1	2
1	2		3
2		3	1
3	1	2	

Skyscrapers 6

3	1	2	
1	2		3
	3	1	2
2		3	1

Skyscrapers 7

	4	1	3	2
3		4	2	1
1	3	2		4
4	2	3	1	
2	1		4	3

Skyscrapers 8

3			1	2
1	2	3		
	1	2		3
	3	1	2	
2			3	1

Skyscrapers 9

2	1		3	4	
	4	1		3	2
1	2	3			4
		4	2	1	3
3			4	2	1
4	3	2	1		

Skyscrapers 10

3			2	1	4
1		4	3		2
2	4	3	1		
	2		4	3	1
	1	2		4	3
4	3	1		2	

Mastermind 1
HAG

Mastermind 2
HEAD

Mastermind 3
THUS

Mastermind 4
WORM

Mastermind 5
DEAL

Mastermind 6
LION

Mastermind 7
SHIRT

Mastermind 8
WHARF

Mastermind 9
ZEBRA

Mastermind 10
GRAPE

Kakuro 1

Kakuro 2

Kakuro 3

Kakuro 4

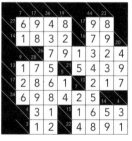

Kakuro 5

Kakuro 6

Kakuro 7

Kakuro 8

Kakuro 9

Kakuro 10

Masyu 1

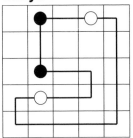

Masyu 2

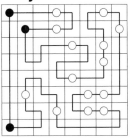

Masyu 3

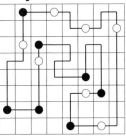

Masyu 4

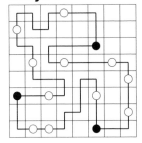

Masyu 5

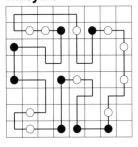

Masyu 6

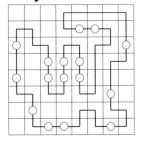

Masyu 7

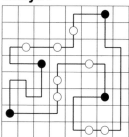

Masyu 8

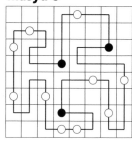

Masyu 9

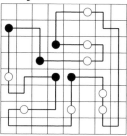

Masyu 10

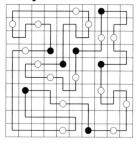

Masyu 11

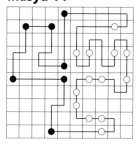

Masyu 12

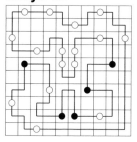

Masyu 13

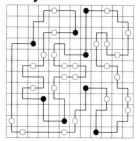

Odd One Out 1

SHIRT. The other words form phrases with the word hand: BACK HAND, RIGHT HAND, FREE HAND, HAND PUPPET, HOUR HAND, HAND TOWEL, HAND BRAKE, UPPER HAND.

Odd One Out 2

MARYLAND. The other words are all street names on a standard Monopoly board.

Odd One Out 3

DIANA. The other words are names of Greek gods (Diana is the Roman equivalent of Artemis).

Odd One Out 4

24. The other numbers are the product of exactly two prime numbers.

Odd One Out 5

BL. All of the other letters form words when you place ORE at the end: BEFORE, ADORE, SHORE, STORE, ENCORE, SCORE, IGNORE, GALORE.

Odd One Out 6

SPHERE. The other words (once anagrammed) form the name of 2-dimensional geometric shapes: PENTAGON, TRAPEZOID, NONAGON, RHOMBUS, CIRCLE, ELLIPSE, SQUARE, TRIANGLE. SPHERE is 3-dimensional.

Odd One Out 7

WHITE. The other words (once their vowels were added back to them) are found in a standard 8-crayon box of Crayola crayons: GREEN, BLUE, VIOLET, RED, BLACK, BROWN, ORANGE, YELLOW.

Odd One Out 8

LIGHT YEAR. The other words (once decoded by replacing 1->A, 2->B, etc.) are units of time: HOUR, DAY, MINUTE, YEAR, MONTH, SECOND, JIFFY, DECADE.

Odd One Out 9

RAPTORS. The other words (once decoded by shifting each letter back 1 letter in the alphabet) are the names of NFL teams: COWBOYS, BRONCOS, JETS, PACKERS, FALCONS, EAGLES, BEARS, LIONS.

Odd One Out 10

SPIN. The other words (once decoded by replacing 1->A, 2->B, etc. from the GRID SUMS problems and reversing the text) are terms related to *The Wizard of Oz*: OIL, DOG, LION, GALE, ROAD, RUBY, WITCH, BRAIN, SHOE.

Exercise Your Mind at American Mensa

At American Mensa, we love puzzles. In fact, we have events—large and small—centered around games and puzzles.

Of course, with tens of thousands of members and growing, we're much more than that, with members aged 2 to 102 and from all walks of life. Our one shared trait might be one you share too: high intelligence, measured in the top 2 percent of the general public in a standardized test.

Get-togethers with other Mensans—from small pizza nights up to larger events like our annual Mind Games—are always stimulating and fun. Roughly 130 Special Interest Groups (we call them SIGs) offer the best of the real and virtual worlds. Highlighting the Mensa newsstand is our award-winning magazine, *Mensa Bulletin*, which stimulates the curious mind with unique features that add perspective to our fast-paced world.

And then there are the practical benefits of membership, such as exclusive offers through our partners and member discounts on magazine subscriptions, online shopping, and financial services.

Find out how to qualify or take our practice test at americanmensa.org/join.